# THE NEED TO KNOW LIBRARY™

# EVERYTHING YOU NEED TO KNOW ABOUT
# FREE SPEECH

DON RAUF

Rosen
YA™

New York

Published in 2019 by The Rosen Publishing Group, Inc.
29 East 21st Street, New York, NY 10010

**Library of Congress Cataloging-in-Publication Data**

Names: Rauf, Don, author.
Title: Everything you need to know about free speech / Don Rauf.
Description: New York : Rosen Publishing, 2019. | Series: The need to know library | Includes bibliographical references and index. | Audience: Grades 7–12.
Identifiers: LCCN 2017050393| ISBN 9781508179191 (library bound) | ISBN 9781508179283 (pbk.)
Subjects: LCSH: Freedom of speech—United States—Juvenile literature. | Freedom of speech—United States—History—Juvenile literature. | Censorship—United States—Juvenile literature.
Classification: LCC KF4772 .R38 2018 | DDC 323.440973—dc23
LC record available at https://lccn.loc.gov/2017050393

*Manufactured in the United States of America*

**On the cover:** A protester exercises her right to free speech by protesting an appearance by President Donald Trump at a meeting of the American Israeli Public Affairs Committee (AIPAC) on March 21, 2016, in Washington, DC.

# CONTENTS

# INTRODUCTION

Duto uring the 2016–2017 season, football player Colin Kaepernick made headlines when he went down on one knee during the national anthem as a silent protest against police brutality and to show support for people of color who are being oppressed in the United States. Some strongly disagreed with his action, believing it showed disrespect for the country. Others strongly supported his action and have taken up his symbolic gesture. No matter what opinion you have, Kaepernick was exercising his right to free speech through this gesture.

Other players followed Kaepernick's lead and have also "taken a knee" at games (although not always during the anthem) They included members of the Miami Dolphins, Dallas Cowboys, New Orleans Saints, Baltimore Ravens, and Buffalo Bills. Performers such as John Legend, David Duchovny, and Olivia Wilde have shared photos of them "taking a knee" as a sign of solidarity with the cause. The gesture gained more widespread attention when President Donald Trump unleashed a Twitter storm lashing out against the practice as unpatriotic.

One of the foundations of America is freedom of speech. Free speech means the free exchange of ideas in order to maintain a healthy democracy. A

As a quarterback for the San Francisco 49ers, Colin Kaepernick (*center*) kneeled during the national anthem. His protest against the oppression of people of color was a form of free speech.

government that suppresses free speech can become more and more controlling and authoritarian. For the most part, the United States gives its citizens the right to express opinions or thoughts without many limits.

That means that opinions that may be unpopular or that you disagree with are allowed. In 2017, white supremacist groups held public demonstrations and marches. These groups often said hateful things about other races and shared beliefs that they should dominate over other people. Because hate groups may have most of their speech protected by law even though it can be repulsive, debate over free speech has grown in recent years. Just how far should free speech go?

The fact is, one of the prices of free speech is dealing with opposing views. While healthy debate can lead to progress, people who clash verbally can sometimes clash physically—harming others and disrupting society as a whole.

Sometimes people may feel they are the target of others' free speech. This can be overwhelming at times and difficult to cope with. Students who feel threatened by attacks should reach out to counselors or law enforcement when needed.

Students, though, should also embrace the power of free speech. Standing up for ideas can help improve education, health care, race relations, employment, and the environment, for example. There are many ways that free speech can cause change and lead to a better world for everybody.

# CHAPTER ONE

# SPEAKING OUT: WHAT'S ALLOWED AND WHAT'S NOT

In June 2017, a rock band was the center of a US Supreme Court case about free speech. An Asian American group with an 80s-style synth pop vibe named itself the Slants. For some Asian Americans, that name had a negative meaning. Front man Simon Tam thought that his band could weaken the offensiveness of the name by embracing it. When the group tried to register the Slants with the US Patent and Trademark Office, however, the government agency blocked the request.

The Patent Office said the band name went against a law that prohibits a trademark that is "disparaging" to a group of people. The band believed this violated their free speech rights and filed a suit. The case went all the way to the Supreme Court, which, in a unanimous decision, sided with the band. Every single member of the court—both conservative and liberal—found that this action by the Patent Office went against the First Amendment's free speech clause.

While speaking about the case in a speech at the University of South Carolina's law school, Supreme

The US Supreme Court unanimously decided that the Slants, seen here performing in 2016, had a free-speech right to use and trademark a name that some found offensive.

Court justice Samuel Alito said that free speech could not be regulated in this way. He defended free speech as "an indispensible component of our system of self-government."

## SOMEONE MAY GET OFFENDED

When you live in a society with free speech—where individuals can say whatever they think and feel—you run the risk of upsetting others. If you voice a strong opinion about government, society, movies, music, or just about anything, you're sure to confront someone who pushes back and disagrees. But, the fact is, you have a right to offend.

Benjamin Franklin, who helped establish the basic principles of American government, explained in his "Apology for Printers," which appeared in the *Pennsylvania Gazette* in 1731, "If all printers were determined not to print anything till they were sure it would offend nobody, there would be very little printed."

Many comedians make their living on this freedom to offend. The late comedian George Carlin said, "It's a comedian's duty to find the line and deliberately cross over it."

## NOT JUST SPEECH

Freedom of speech goes beyond talking—it encompasses a freedom of all expression. In a free society, individuals can publish their ideas in newspapers, in books, in magazines, and online. They can put forth their thoughts in movies, television shows, and radio programs. People can create music and visual art that they wish to make without threat or control from the government.

Our right to express ourselves extends to the clothes we wear—messages and symbols on buttons, armbands, hats, and T-shirts are all protected by the First Amendment. Through our clothing, we can also broadcast our support for a political candidate.

Freedom of speech encompasses all forms of expression. For example, people have a right to express their political beliefs on their clothing, as these men are doing.

## TO TALK OUT OR CHOOSE NOT TO

Overall, freedom of speech protects a citizen's right to say whatever he or she wants. This freedom means people can discuss issues with neighbors and make public speeches about the topics they wish. They can argue and debate freely—and even use insulting language.

This right also means people can come together and voice concerns, as in a protest or a march for a cause. Demonstrations, however, need to happen at appropriate times, with the right permits and protections.

## DEFENDING ALL SPEECH

The American Civil Liberties Union (ACLU) believes in the freedom of all expression and that constitutional rights must apply to even the most unpopular groups if those rights are going to be preserved for everyone. The organization has defended the rights of communists, Nazis, Ku Klux Klan members, accused terrorists, and others who have engaged in truly offensive speech. Because the defense of free speech is an essential part of its mission, the ACLU has been involved in almost all of the landmark speech cases that have reached the US Supreme Court.

In addition, American citizens have the right not to speak. For example, you do not have to participate in the Pledge of Allegiance. Saying the pledge most often comes up with students in schools, and rules regarding freedom of speech in schools can be distinct.

## STILL, FREE EXPRESSION HAS ITS LIMITS

Although the law allows for most forms of free expression, America has its restrictions. For example, you cannot put forth ideas and words to stir up violence or harm toward others. The US government outlaws speech that creates a "clear and present danger," so using words to encourage people to pursue violent actions is a crime.

Also, individuals cannot use words that cause panic and put lives at risk. An example used frequently is falsely yelling "Fire!" in a crowded theater. The First Amendment does not defend this type of reckless speech.

Although our legal system has upheld burning a flag as a form of free speech, burning a draft card is forbidden. (The draft is the compulsory enrollment of men into military service.) During the Vietnam War, thousands of young men burned their draft cards in protest. They defended the action as free speech, but the Supreme Court came down against this. Basically, the ban on card destruction was justified to keep the military registration system operating smoothly.

While language that is offensive may be protected, American laws restrict the use of obscene language and

During the 1960s, some young men burned their draft cards in protest against the Vietnam War. The Supreme Court rejected the claim that this was protected as an act of free speech.

images. Obscene words, images, or actions offend the sexual morality of a given time, place, and population. Some types of obscenity can threaten women and children. In some cases, defining what is obscene and not just offensive can be difficult. Former Supreme Court justice Potter Stewart famously said that's it's hard to explain but "I know it when I see it."

In 1973, the Supreme Court heard the case of *Miller v. California*. Marvin Miller was arrested after sending out a mass mailing about "adult" material. California forbade the distribution of obscene material. Miller thought his First Amendment rights had been violated. The Supreme Court decided that the distribution of obscene material to the public was not protected as free speech. Based on the verdict, the Miller Test for obscenity was established. If a work met all three of the following criteria, it was deemed obscene:

1. The average person, applying contemporary community standards, would find that the work, taken as a whole, appeals to the prurient interest.
2. The work depicts/describes, in a patently offensive way, sexual conduct or excretory functions specifically defined by applicable state law.
3. The work, taken as a whole, lacks serious literary, artistic, political, or scientific value.

The bottom line is you can express just about anything you want in America without being punished by the government, but you need to be aware of a few restrictions.

# CHAPTER TWO

# A COUNTRY BUILT ON FREE THOUGHT

**M**any of the basic freedoms of Americans are enshrined in the First Amendment of the Constitution. It reads:

*Congress shall make no law respecting an establishment of religion, or prohibiting the free exercise thereof; or abridging the freedom of speech, or of the press; or the right of the people peaceably to assemble, and to petition the Government for a redress of grievances.*

## THANK OUR FOUNDING FATHERS

Our country's Founding Fathers included Thomas Jefferson, George Washington, John Adams, Alexander Hamilton, James Madison, and Benjamin Franklin. They had lived under the thumb of an oppressive government. Because they knew that man's natural tendency was to seek concentrated power, they created a country that would limit power in the hands of a few.

## JAMES MADISON: THE AUTHOR OF FREE SPEECH

Though he is also remembered as America's fourth president, James Madison is often referred to as the "Father of the Constitution." He earned this name because of the important roles he played in both the writing and the ratification of this historic document, which became the law of the land in 1788. Under the mentorship of Thomas Jefferson, Madison also drafted most of the ten amendments that make up the Bill of Rights, including the First Amendment.

They wanted a government that would protect the freedoms of its people—not take away those freedoms. They thought that every man had certain natural rights, including the freedom of speech. To assure citizens their rights, the Founding Fathers worked together to create the Constitution and the Bill of Rights (the first ten amendments, which became law in 1791).

## AN EARLY TEST

A major challenge to free speech came up seven years after the Bill of Rights was approved. President John Adams and his Federalist Party held the majority in Congress. They passed the Alien and Sedition Acts with the purpose of making the country more secure from foreign spies and domestic traitors. The

President John Adams signed into law the Alien and Sedition Acts, which restricted speech that was critical of the government.

Sedition Act restricted free speech, making it illegal to publish anything "false, scandalous, or malicious" against the federal government.

Under this law, one man was arrested for posting a hand-painted sign reading "Downfall to the Tyrants of America." Yet another was imprisoned for expressing his wish that John Adams be struck in the seat of his pants with a wadding of cannon fire.

The Democratic-Republican Party, led by Thomas Jefferson and James Madison, argued that these actions violated free speech rights. Two years after the introduction of the Alien and Sedition Acts, Thomas Jefferson was elected president and enforcement of these acts came to an end. As he wrote in a letter to the doctor James Currie, "Our liberty depends on the freedom of the press, and that cannot be limited without being lost."

# A FIGHT FOR MORALITY AND PATRIOTISM

In 1873, Congress passed the Comstock Act, or the act for the "Suppression of Trade in, and Circulation of, Obscene Literature and Articles of Immoral Use." The act prohibited distributing any "article of an immoral nature, or any drug or medicine, or any article what-ever for the prevention of contraception or procuring of abortion" through the US mail or across state lines. Many criticized the law as a strike against free speech, but the law was upheld on the grounds that the First Amendment does not protect obscene speech.

In 1989, the Supreme Court ruled that the act of burning the American flag is a form of symbolic speech and protected by the First Amendment.

In 1897, Illinois, Pennsylvania, and South Dakota became the first states to ban the desecration of the flag. The ban partially came in response to those who would post an advertisement on the flag and wave it around. Years later, the Supreme Court would rule that desecrating the flag was a form of free expression that was protected by the First Amendment.

## THE SUPREME COURT SHAPES THE LAW

The US Supreme Court has defined what exactly protected free speech means in this country. The court serves as the final judge for cases involving the laws of Congress. It tries to ensure that each American citizen receives equal justice under law. As the interpreter of the Constitution, the Supreme Court ultimately decides what is legal and what is not.

An early Supreme Court case about free speech came in 1919, when judges ruled that the country could limit speech during wartime. The Sedition Act of 1918 was similar in some regards to the Sedition Act under John Adams. This law prohibited people from taking any effort that went against the government's participation in World War I. When the pacifist labor organizer Eugene V. Debs made an anti-war speech in Ohio in 1918, he was arrested and sentenced to ten years in prison because he disobeyed the Sedition Act. Debs's case went all the way to the Supreme Court, which ruled against him, saying Debs obstructed the war effort. In 1921, Congress repealed this Sedition Act and Debs went free.

## A CLEAR AND PRESENT DANGER

In another related case in 1919, the Supreme Court ruled that the socialist Charles Schenck was not protected by the First Amendment when he distributed materials that interfered with military recruitment. Justice Oliver Wendell Holmes argued that during wartime Schenk's actions were dangerous—like shouting "Fire!" in a crowded theater. The government could legally restrict speech when the words create a "clear and present danger." This concept of "clear and present danger" continues to be the test today to decide if certain free expression is allowed by the First Amendment.

Eugene V. Debs was arrested for speaking out against World War I. The Supreme Court agreed that he was obstructing the war effort.

The Alien Registration Act of 1940 made it illegal to express thoughts about the overthrow of the US government. The government used the law to prosecute anyone affiliated with the American Communist Party. In 1951, the Supreme Court said the law was constitutional, but later many of the convictions were reversed.

Another important free speech case was *Chaplinsky v. State of New Hampshire* in 1942. The court established that "fighting words" did not enjoy First Amendment protections. These are words that might spark violence or lead to injury. Still, fighting words can be hard to define. The court has refined the meaning through different decisions over the years. In 1971, the judges ruled that offensive language did not constitute "fighting words." So speech that is lewd, vulgar, or profane is protected.

## FOUL LANGUAGE SHALL NOT BE BROADCAST

In 1978, the Supreme Court decided that the Federal Communications Commission (FCC) could restrict broadcast television and radio from transmitting indecent content. Rules about indecency and profanity, however, do not apply to cable, satellite TV, and satellite radio because they are subscription services. After public uproar about Howard Stern and other radio show hosts using very explicit language, the FCC tightened the rules about using language about sex and bodily functions on radio, television, and telephone services.

Congress established rules regarding indecency on the internet in 1996, but a Supreme Court case struck down these restrictions saying they violated the First Amendment's guarantee of free speech.

# MYTHS AND FACTS

**MYTH:** All speech is protected in the United States.

**FACT:** There are some limits to speech. Most of the limits concern speech that poses a clear and present danger to people.

**MYTH:** Hate speech is not allowed in this country.

**FACT:** The Supreme Court has ruled that even hate speech is protected by the First Amendment unless it makes a direct personal threat of immediate violence or is shown to be truly harmful or dangerous in some other way.

**MYTH:** Schools follow the same free speech rules as everyone else.

**FACT:** Schools have been able to set some limits on speech that interferes with the learning environment or is seen as harmful to the students.

# CHAPTER THREE

# SCHOOLS PLAY BY THEIR OWN RULES

**W**hile the United States has laws about free speech, schools set their own regulations. Sometimes a school's policy to create an environment that is safe, orderly, and conducive to learning comes up against the laws that guarantee free speech.

In 1943, several students and their parents argued for their right to not say the Pledge of Allegiance in the school. They were Jehovah's Witnesses who believed in only pledging allegiance to God, not to the flag or anything else. This was during World War II, and the West Virginia State Board of Education felt it vital for the country that all citizens show their national pride by pledging allegiance.

The students, however, said that refraining from the pledge was within both their rights to freedom of religion and expression. The high court agreed that school administrators could not force students to do something that went against their religious beliefs. This was a case of free speech defending an individual's right not to speak just as much as his or her right to speak.

## TAKING A POLITICAL STAND

In 1965, thirteen-year-old Mary Beth Tinker and a small group of her friends wore black armbands to their school in Des Moines, Iowa, as a protest against the Vietnam War. The armbands were symbols of mourning for those who had died on both sides in the long-running battle. The school, however, decided to forbid the practice on the grounds that this demonstration interfered with carrying out school activities. Tinker persisted. The eighth grader thought it was within her First Amendment rights to do so. When she wore the

Although their school tried to block Mary Beth Tinker and her brother, Paul, from wearing black armbands to protest the Vietnam War, the Supreme Court decided it was within their constitutional rights.

black armband again to school, she was suspended. She and several other students were told that they simply could not come back to school wearing the bands. When they returned to school grounds, they took a new tactic and wore black clothing the rest of the year as a protest.

Tinker legally challenged the school decision and the case went to the highest court. Four years after the incident, the Supreme Court ruled that students have First Amendment rights. In his decision on the case, Justice Abe Fortas wrote that both students and teachers "do not shed their constitutional rights to freedom of speech or expression at the schoolhouse gate." Still there were limits. The court established that students could not "materially and substantially" disrupt classes or other school activities. It was decided that wearing a symbol did not do that.

## STEPPING OVER THE LINE

In other free speech cases involving students, the court decided that a student did go too far and did cause a disruption. In 1983, senior Matthew Fraser of Washington State made a speech at a high school assembly nominating a friend for student government. Because the speech was loaded with sexual innuendo, the school suspended him on the grounds that his vulgar and offensive words were disruptive to the orderly proceedings at the school.

With the help of the ACLU, Fraser sued the school, contending that its action went against his constitutional right to free speech. The court, however, decided that the students could be silenced under some circumstances—schools had a responsibility to instill civility and the right to maintain socially appropriate behavior.

During the Olympic Torch Relay through Juneau, Alaska, on January 24, 2002, senior Joseph Frederick of Juneau-Douglas High School unfurled a banner that read "Bong Hits 4 Jesus." Principal Deborah Morse thought the words were inappropriate for a school-supervised event because the words might encourage illegal drug use. She asked Frederick to put the banner away, but he refused. She confiscated the banner and suspended him for ten days. Frederick sued the school.

In general, students have constitutional rights to freedom of speech unless those forms of expression are disruptive to the school environment.

At first, a district court found in favor of the school. Frederick appealed to the US Court of Appeals for the Ninth Circuit, which reversed the decision. That court said Frederick's banner should have been allowed because it did not cause a disturbance. The school then took the case to the country's highest court. Ultimately, the Supreme Court decided that the school had the right to curb Frederick's speech. It said that a school has a authority to discourage drug use, and Frederick's message promoted drug intake. Although students have some rights to free speech in school, the Supreme Court has set limits.

## SCHOOL DRESS CODES

The day before Violet Redwine was due to graduate from high school in Lexington, North Carolina, she was kicked out. Her dress was half an inch too short.

Different schools have different dress codes establishing what a student can and cannot wear on school grounds. Schools say that such codes help build a safe, disciplined learning environment so students will not be distracted from their studies. Most states have laws that let schools establish their own dress codes. Dress codes can apply to grooming, too—some schools have set regulations on hair length, jewelry, and piercings.

A school is within its rights to ban clothes that expose too much skin or undergarments—such as shirts that expose midriffs, short skirts, or baggy pants that show underwear. These clothes may be seen as vulgar or ob-

Although public schools can have their own dress codes, students have a right to wear garments connected to their religious beliefs, such as the Islamic headscarf called the hijab.

scene and prohibited because they draw focus away from classroom activities. Schools may restrict gang-related clothing or clothing with provocative messages.

The ACLU says that as a general rule, public schools cannot bar you from wearing clothing simply because they disapprove of the message that the clothing conveys. Students must also be able to wear clothing to express religious beliefs—such as a headscarf, cross necklace, turban, or yarmulke.

Schools have tried to control what students can wear in their yearbook photos as well. In some cases, the

## STOP THE STUDENT PRESSES

Another area of free speech in the schools is with the student newspaper. In 1983, students enrolled in a journalism class at Hazelwood East High School in Missouri submitted articles about divorce and teen pregnancy to be published in the *Spectrum*, the school paper. The principal had concerns about how the articles were written and deemed them to be inappropriate.

The articles did not go to press and the student editors sued the school, saying they had been inappropriately censored. The court decided in favor of the school because the paper was sponsored by the school, so administrators could decide if the contents related to educational concerns or went against civilized order in the school. The decision highlighted the point that if the paper were not school-sponsored, the students would have greater freedom of speech.

ACLU has successfully challenged these cases on the grounds of free speech. For example, a school banned a student from wearing medieval clothing and a prop broadsword in the yearbook, but the ACLU successfully challenged this restriction.

## A WATCHFUL EYE ON THE WEB

The internet has introduced new questions about how schools monitor their students. In today's world, many schools have disciplined students for things they have written online. The issue of internet use again raises the question: where is the line between free speech and disruption for the school?

As a thirteen-year-old sixth grader in Minnesota in 2012, Riley Stratton posted on her Facebook page that she hated her hall monitor because she was "mean." When school administrators heard about her online comments, they called her into their office and forced her to turn over her Facebook and email account passwords in front of a sheriff's deputy. They suspended her for her words on Facebook. The ACLU filed a suit against the district, saying it had violated her rights. The school

For schools, social media has posed new challenges about free speech. Do educational institutions have the right to discipline students who post messages that might be viewed as harmful?

district wound up paying Stratton and her family $70,000 in damages and then rewriting its rules for when a school could search a student's social media or email accounts that are created off of school grounds.

Charles Samuelson, executive director of the ACLU in Minnesota said, "There may be times when it is appropriate for schools to intervene, but only in extreme circumstances where there are true threats or safety risks."

In the same school district, an honors student who was also captain of the high school football and basketball teams posted a two word tweet—"Actually, yeah"—that got him suspended. He said it was intended to be a joke about making out with a teacher. The tweet got him suspended for two months. The student took the case to a district court, which found that the student had been unjustly suspended and his free speech rights may have been violated because the comment was made outside of school hours, off school grounds, and without the use of school property. The school settled the case for $425,000.

## REAL CONCERNS

Schools can have legitimate concerns about cyberbullies online and posts that indicate a direct threat to students' safety. As a growing number of schools have punished students for their online comments, the question is where is the line between free speech and a "clear and present danger."

Mary Beth Tinker, who fought for her right to wear a black armband in the 1960s in protest of the Vietnam War, has remained an advocate for student free speech rights. In an article in the *Atlantic* magazine, she wrote:

> *The digital age, with its wonderful capacity to democratize speech, is so important to students' rights, but also carries new and interesting threats to students' rights. If we don't encourage young people to use their First Amendment rights, our society is deprived of their creativity, energy, and new ideas. This is a huge loss, and also a human rights abuse.*

# CHAPTER FOUR

# CHALLENGING CENSORSHIP

**E**ven though free speech is protected in the United States in many ways, people continue to find ways to block free expression through censorship. The ACLU defines censorship as the suppression of words, images, or ideas that are "offensive." Censorship can come from broadcast companies, publishers, local governments, libraries, schools, religious groups, and other organizations that make decisions about what they think the public should see or not see. Censorship can apply to comic books, posters, billboards, television shows, movies, radio programs, paintings, theatrical productions, books, magazines, and other forms of expression that surround you every day.

## IS YOUR LIFE BEING CENSORED?

Censorship can be hard to spot at times because it can happen without much notice. For example, a school may decide not to stock certain books on its shelves because it deems them inappropriate. Students and parents may not give much thought to materials that are not there. Whether censorship is right or wrong is a matter of opinion. You may agree with some types of censorship. Some believe that it is right to stop children from hearing or seeing inappropriate things. Others, because of their religious views, may object to materials that teach Darwin's theory of evolution.

## TAKING ACTION

Who should be able to decide what materials are censored? Should the government and schools decide what is appropriate and what is not? These are

This protester in Texas believes that schools should not be censored in their teaching of evolution.

questions you have to ask when considering censorship.

To fight against censorship you disagree with, the American Library Association recommends that you:

**Stay informed.** Read up on censorship issues. Find out what books and other materials are in your library and which are not. Learn what the policies are for challenging decisions related to censorship.

**Get involved.** Go to school board meetings. Volunteer at your library. Create an event to discuss issues.

**Speak out.** If you feel strongly about a topic, write letters to the editor, the library director, local politicians, school officials, media companies, or others that control access to information. Talk to neighbors and friends about your concerns.

**Know your rights.** Just because materials may be censored does not mean you do not have the right to access them. You may be within your rights to view materials that are being blocked.

Many actions have been taken over the years to censor material. Learning the history of censorship can help you recognize it when it happens again.

## BANISHED BOOKS

Many books that are now considered classics have been labeled unacceptable by some libraries and schools because of sexual content. They include *Catcher in the Rye* by J. D. Salinger, *Beloved* by Toni Morrison, *Leaves of Grass* by Walt Whitman, *Native Son* by Richard Wright, *The Scarlet Letter* by Nathaniel Hawthorne, and *A Street Car Named Desire* by Tennessee Williams. *Grapes of Wrath* by John Steinbeck and *Ulysses* by James Joyce were also subject to censorship.

Mark Twain's *Adventures of Huckleberry Finn* has been the target of many bans for multiple reasons. Soon after it was published in 1884, librarians in Concord, Massachusetts, blocked the book, finding the story of the high-spirited white boy and his runaway slave friend, Jim, to be offensive, immoral, and sacrilegious. In the 1950s, the NAACP objected to students learning the novel because of the depiction of Jim and language used to describe him. In 2015, Friends' Central School in Philadelphia banned the book from the curriculum for students ages sixteen and seventeen because its use of racial epithets upset people.

In October 2017, the school board in Biloxi, Mississippi, pulled *To Kill a Mockingbird* from its eighth grade reading list, citing language that made people feel "uncomfortable." Are there any books that might be blocked from your school shelves?

*Huckleberry Finn* is considered a classic American novel, yet it has been banned by schools and libraries over the decades.

## EVEN SUPERMAN WAS FORBIDDEN

In America, comic books were subject to burnings in the 1940s and 1950s. The extreme measure started in 1948 when Dr. Fredric Wertham, a noted German psychiatrist working in Harlem, said that comics led to delinquency and made young men abnormally aggressive. Superhero comics and horror comics were especially to blame. Wertham believed superhero comics gave boys a dangerous superhero complex that made them think they could do anything.

His campaign against comics influenced many towns to organize comic book burnings before the minds of their youngsters were corrupted. In Binghamton, New York, "civic-minded" parents gathered more than two thousand comics and set fire to them in 1948. Similar public burnings were held in Spencer, West

In the 1950s and 1960s, some Americans thought comic books were a bad influence on young people. A few communities even organized public burnings to keep impressionable youth from viewing them.

Virginia, where a 6-foot (1.8-meter) high pile was set ablaze surrounded by a big crowd.

Today, depictions of zombies and werewolves are so common that it may be hard to imagine a time when the Comics Magazine Association of America banned such illustrations. In 1954, the group came up with the Comics Code, censoring images of ghouls, werewolves, zombies, and other characters considered inappropriate for young minds. The code encouraged storylines about respect for authority and the value of marriage. By the early 1970s, the code began to fade, especially after Stan Lee at Marvel comics published a Spiderman series without the official seal of approval.

## LIGHTS! ACTION! CENSORSHIP!

Today, some people uphold that the rating systems used by parents so they can decide what movies and TV shows are appropriate for their kids are a form of censorship. Others believe that the system (G, PG, R, etc.) is a good way to help parents determine what their kids should view. Censorship in the film industry arrived almost as soon as it was invented. In 1896, Thomas Edison's *The Kiss*—all of eighteen seconds long and showing a peck on the cheek—was condemned by some as a threat to morality. Chicago enacted the first film censorship law in American in 1907, and many cities and states followed suit. In 1915, the Supreme Court ruled that movies are not protected by the First Amendment, and local governments can set their own controls.

Featuring cross-dressing men, *Some Like It Hot* became a hit without a seal of approval from the Production Code.

In 1934, under pressure from different groups, the Motion Picture Producers and Distributors of America (MPPDA) put together a list of dos and don'ts that films had to meet to pass moral standards so films would be wholesome. Members of the MPPDA owned many of the theaters in the country, so they wanted films that met their standards. For example, films couldn't show suggestive dancing or overly passionate kissing. The cartoon character Betty Boop started wearing longer skirts.

In 1952, the Supreme Court ruled for the first time that "motion pictures are a significant medium for the communication of ideas" and entitled to First Amendment protection. In 1959, the comedy *Some Like It Hot* depicted men dressing as women. Released without a code approval from the MPPDA's Production Code Administration, the movie went on to be a success, weakening the power of the MPPDA code.

# POISON TO THE EARS

It might be hard to imagine having other people determine what music you can or cannot listen too. But like movies and other media, music has also been the target of censorship. Rap and hip-hop lyrics have been blamed for increased gang violence. Sexually explicit

## FOLK MUSIC AND ELVIS WERE ONCE RESTRICTED

In the 1950s, the Weavers were a folk music group that became popular singing old standards like "Good Night Irene." When the public found out that members supported pacifism and expressed support for prolabor ideas and the Communist Party, they were blacklisted. TV shows canceled their appearances, clubs would not hire them, and their record label dropped them. They had the freedom to express themselves, but when a large population turned against them, they felt their freedom of expression crushed. The band disbanded.

*The Ed Sullivan Show* would only broadcast Elvis Presley singing from the waist up because many thought his hip movements sparked inappropriate feelings in teenage fans. In the 1960s, radio stations across the America banned "I Can't Get No Satisfaction" by the Rolling Stones because it had sexually suggestive lyrics. These are just a few memorable examples of music-related censorship, but broadcasters have blocked many different songs over the decades.

lyrics in rock and rap are thought by some to have a negative impact on women, children, and young adults. Throughout history, different groups have fought to block music that they thought was harmful to their children or to society.

In 1984, the Parents Music Resource Center was formed by parents who were disturbed that their kids were listening to Prince, Madonna, AC/DC, Cyndi Lauper, and other music they labeled as "porn rock." Their efforts led the record industry to slap a label on CDs that included language and content thought to be inappropriate to kids. The label read PARENTAL ADVISORY: EXPLICIT CONTENT.

This label today is still incorporated into both physical and digital artwork for some albums. The label has backfired in some ways. Many young people want what they can't have—so many albums with the label have

## CENSORSHIP ON THE INTERNET

The ACLU argues that the internet is a vast free speech zone where your First Amendment rights should be protected. However, the companies that control internet access have been deciding what content should or should not be seen. For example, Google and GoDaddy refused to host a neo-Nazi website, making an effort to block hate groups on the internet. Spotify is refusing to play music "that favors hatred or incites violence against race, religion, sexuality or the like." Even OKCupid deleted the profile of a white supremacist.

sold more because of it. In the digital age, censoring artistic materials has become harder than ever.

## KNOWING YOUR RIGHTS IN THE MODERN AGE

In the internet age, we have even more ways to express ourselves. It has made it easier to post thoughts in haste that we might regret later or not necessarily mean. In the past few years, the world has seen many terrorist attacks. That has made the authorities extra wary about any potential speech or writing that could be seen as harmful.

While some people support Parental Advisory labels on music, others think they suppress free expression.

## A THREAT OR SELF-EXPRESSION

While in high school in Methuen, Massachusetts, Cameron D'Ambrosio was known as a quiet, normal kid. The teenager was also an aspiring rapper going by the name CammyDee. In 2013, he posted lyrics on Facebook that he said expressed some inner anger. He referred to a Boston bombing and said that he'd kill people and beat every "murder charge that comes across me." People in Massachusetts were especially sensitive to D'Ambrosio's violent lyrics just a short time after the Boston Marathon bombing that April. When someone notified the police about his postings, he was arrested and held on $1 million dollars bail for making terrorist threats. Charges were dropped after he spent a month in jail.

D'Ambrosio may have shown poor judgment in posting such provocative words. His case shows some of the limits of free speech and how language can trigger action to be taken to prevent any possible harm. It also shows how easy it is for information to spread on the internet and the lack of thought people may put into posting things online.

Students today have to ask themselves: will my words be taken as a threat that could cause serious danger? Sometimes, it's wise to take a pause before posting anything. People can often regret what they post in a moment of anger. After stepping away from the computer screen for a break, a person may see how his or her comments could be an overreaction or seen as causing trouble.

# CHAPTER FIVE

# TAKING A STAND AND CONFRONTING OTHERS

Freedom of speech is not only about how we express ourselves to the world, it's also about what we experience from others who are sharing their

Living in a society with free speech requires tolerating the opinions and thoughts of others even if they are upsetting or if you disagree with them.

thoughts. Some expressions of belief and opinion may seem more outrageous than others, but just because you disagree or feel deeply upset, angry, or hurt by someone else's thoughts, this does not mean that those ideas are illegal or not allowed.

Many Americans grow up with an ingrained reverence for the country's flag. They believe the flag should never be harmed. On August 22, 1984, Gregory Lee Johnson protested the two presidential candidates that year by burning a flag. The action led to his arrest. In time, however, his case made it to the Supreme Court, which ruled that flag burning is a legal form of protest protected by the First Amendment.

## RACIST AND HOSTILE ATTITUDES ALLOWED

Many disagree with laws that uphold free expression that is hateful toward others. A significant Supreme Court decision on this topic came with the case *Brandenburg v. Ohio*. In 1964, Clarence Brandenburg organized a Ku Klux Klan (KKK) rally. Formed in 1865, the KKK has the distinction of being one of America's oldest hate groups. It has taken a stance against blacks, Jews, immigrants, gays and lesbians, and, until recently, Catholics. At Brandenburg's rally, men dressed in white hoods and robes, burned a cross, and made speeches talking about vengeance against blacks and Jews. Brandenburg was arrested for breaking the law in Ohio, but his case went all the way to the Supreme

## EXTREME EXPRESSION—STILL PROTECTED

More than 4,400 US soldiers died during the War in Iraq. In 2006, when Lance Corporal Matthew Snyder was killed, he was brought back to the United States for a funeral to honor his life. Members of the Westboro Baptist Church believed that soldiers were dying for the sins of America. They protested outside the cemetery during his funeral. One sign at the protest read "Thank God for dead soldiers." The Southern Poverty Law Center labeled the Westboro Baptist Church as a "hate group." Snyder's family sued the church for emotional distress and other issues. In 2010, the Supreme Court ultimately ruled in favor of the church in an 8–1 decision. Because the church protest related to a public issue and was on public property, the court found that the action was protected by freedom of speech laws even though it was repugnant and distasteful.

Court. The court ruled that free speech laws protected the KKK rally because the event did not incite or produce imminent lawless action.

## CONFRONTING AND COPING WITH OPPOSITION

When you speak up for ideas you believe in, you may confront those who disagree with you. Or you may hear of demonstrations that you disagree with. People have a right to respectfully disagree, but conflicting groups may face off against each other, leading to shouting matches and possible violence.

That's what happened in August 2017 when counterdemonstrators faced off against white supremacists who were marching in Charlottesville, Virginia. Both sides had a right to be there and exercise their free speech rights. Counterprotesters had the right to push back against views they found reprehensible. Many protests have been held in the United States since the election of Donald Trump with conflicting groups arguing their opinions on the environment, health care, education, taxes, and other topics of public concern. While people may be vocal about

The US Constitution guarantees the right to peaceful assembly, which means citizens can gather and demonstrate their support or opposition to public policy.

their opinions, it is important not to physically harm anyone.

Some speech might be hateful—racist, bigoted, sexist, or homophobic, for example. But it is allowed under free speech laws unless it is harassing or threatening. To deal with hate speech and other expression you disagree with, you can try one of the following approaches:

**Confronting.** The ACLU argues that more speech is the answer to confronting negative attitudes. Counterprotesting is legal.

**Conversing.** Talking about issues in a civil way—to friends, family, and anyone you disagree with—can lead to change. African American Daryl Davis had spent thirty years befriending members of the KKK. By talking to them, he has convinced two hundred members to quit the hate group.

**Counseling.** You may be deeply offended by some speech. If you are having trouble dealing with hurtful speech, seek out others to talk over the issue. If you are feeling depressed or doubting your self-worth after confronting hateful points of view, school and private counselors may be able to help.

## PUTTING FREE SPEECH TO GOOD USE

If you do have strong beliefs or political opinions and want to speak up for changes in the world, you should feel free to do so. Spouting your thoughts on Facebook pages and in "comments" sections online is fine, but there are ways that your words and actions may have more power to produce change.

In 2014, hundreds of students in Jefferson County, Colorado, staged a walkout to protest proposed changes in AP history instruction that would emphasize respect for authority over civil disobedience. Students might protest any topic, such as making college more affordable, introducing more recycling in the school, stopping bullying, or improving cafeteria lunches.

There are many ways to exercise your rights for free speech. For example:

**Defend the free press.** Some people in power will condemn the free press. They might try to convince others that the press is false. The more the press is condemned by people in power, the harder it is to criticize and cause change. The press is necessary for people to share opinions. To keep free speech alive, support newspapers and other media that help spread diverse thoughts and ideas.

**Ask your representative to support the First Amendment.** If you see attacks against free speech, contact your representatives in Congress and ask them to take a strong stance to defend free expression.

**Launch or support a petition.** Your ideas can gain more power if others support them. A petition gathers signatures of others who agree with a position. The freedom to petition the government to express grievances is written in the First Amendment. In 2014, Sara Wolff led a campaign signed by more than 265,000 people, urging Congress to help people with disabilities take more control of their finances. The petition helped push Congress to pass a disabilities rights act that did just that.

One effective way to have your opinion matter is to start a letter-writing campaign or organize a petition to seek change.

**Write a letter.** A letter to the press, TV stations, radio stations, or political figures can help nudge change forward. Well-written letters stimulate debate among politicians and the public. Amnesty International has led effective letter-writing campaigns that have led to the release of prisoners they believe have been unjustly jailed. "When ordinary people stand together and send a clear message demanding governments fulfill their duty to protect and uphold people's human rights we can achieve fantastic results," said Salil Shetty, Amnesty International's secretary general.

**Join or mount a protest.** Another right guaranteed by the First Amendment is to peacefully assemble. Gathering like-minded voices together in a public protest can gain notice and bring about change. On August 26, 1963, Martin Luther King Jr. led more than two hundred thousand Americans in a march on Washington, DC, to support racial equality and justice. He delivered his famous "I Have a Dream" speech there. Congress passed the Civil Rights Act the following year.

## EXERCISING YOUR RIGHTS

You have the right to speak out, but sometimes others will try to stop you. As a student, you should know school policy regarding the ways you are permitted to express yourself. What are school regulations regarding assemblies, theatrical productions, the newspaper, demonstrations, and other public forms of expression? Some of the ways you might want to express yourself may be allowed if you follow school rules. The key is to not be disruptive. Usually a school must allow protests held before or after class and in a safe location that doesn't block entries and exits. Be aware of being too loud and disturbing the peace.

If you are exercising free speech in a public place, make sure you have any necessary permits. Check if your community has a free speech zone (a public area set aside for protesting). The government can't prohibit marches on public sidewalks or streets or rallies in most public parks or plazas. The ACLU says if you hold

The Women's March on January 21, 2017, was one of the largest single-day demonstrations in US history, with an estimated tally of more than four million participants nationwide.

a small rally in a public park or march on the sidewalk and obey traffic laws, you generally won't need a permit. If you are organizing some sort of public demonstration, the key is always to make sure it is not disruptive. Carefully consider the where, when, and how. In a public setting, you have the right to set up a table, distribute materials, and stop people and engage them in conversation.

Standing up for what you believe in is not always easy. Throughout history, great people have taken a stand for their beliefs and often suffered at the hands of those who disagreed or felt threatened by those beliefs. To live in a better world, we sometimes must struggle and make the effort to speak out for what's right.

As author Suzy Kassem wrote on her blog,

> *Stand up to hypocrisy. If you don't, the hypocrites will teach. Stand up to ignorance, because if you don't, the ignorant will run free to spread ignorance like a disease. Stand up for truth. If you don't, then there is no truth to your existence. If you don't stand up for all that is right, then understand that you are part of the reason why there is so much wrong in the world.*

# 10 GREAT QUESTIONS TO ASK A LAWYER

1. Why is the right to free expression at the core of democracy? How does it improve society?
2. What are the dangers of suppressing free speech and how is free speech being suppressed in America?
3. What are the freedoms guaranteed by the First Amendment?
4. What are examples of free speech zones (public areas set aside for political protesting)?
5. Do you think there should be absolute free speech or should there be some limits?
6. Are there some cases about free speech in which it is hard to decide what is right or wrong?
7. Should students have the same free speech rights as adults?
8. What Supreme Court cases on free speech do you disagree with?
9. Do you think censorship is sometimes OK? When is it OK?
10. Does the internet have total freedom of speech?

**abridge**  To shorten.

**blacklist**  To put a person on a list of those who are barred from employment or punished because they hold opinions considered undesirable.

**censorship**  The suppression or prohibition of any parts of books, films, news, or other forms of expression that are considered obscene, politically unacceptable, or a threat to security.

**compulsory**  Required by law.

**democratize**  To make something available to all people.

**disparaging**  Demeaning; belittling.

**grievance**  A real or imagined cause for complaint or protest, especially unfair treatment.

**intervene**  To get involved in a difficult situation or conflict in order to influence what happens.

**obscene**  Offensive or disgusting by accepted standards of morality and decency.

**oppressive**  Unjustly cruel or harsh.

**petition**  To make a formal written request, typically one signed by many people, appealing to authority with respect to a particular cause.

**redress**  To set right.

**repeal**  To end an established law so it is no longer valid.

**sedition**  Speech or conduct that incites people to rebel against the authority of a state or monarch.

**unanimous**  With no disagreement.

American Civil Liberties Union (ACLU)
125 Broad Street, 18th Floor
New York, NY 10004
(212) 549-2500
Website: http://www.aclu.org
Facebook: @aclu
Twitter: @ACLU
The ACLU works to defend and preserve the individual
    rights and liberties guaranteed by the Constitution
    and laws of the United States.

Canadian Civil Liberties Association (CCLA)
90 Eglinton Avenue E, Suite 900
Toronto, ON M4P 2Y3
Canada
(416) 363-0321
Website: http://www.ccla.org
Facebook and Twitter: @cancivlib
The CCLA is dedicated to fighting for the civil liberties,
    human rights, and democratic freedoms of all peo-
    ple across Canada.

Centre for Free Expression
Rogers Communications Centre
80 Gould Street
Toronto, ON M5B 2M7
Canada
(416) 979-5000, ext. 6396

Website: http://www.cfe.ryerson.ca
Facebook: @CentreforFreeExpresssion
Twitter: @RyersonCFE
The Centre for Free Expression is a hub for public education, research, and advocacy on free expression and the public's right to know. The group collaborates with academic and community-based organizations across Canada and internationally.

Constitutional Rights Foundation (CRF)
601 South Kingsley Drive
Los Angeles, CA 90005
(213) 487-5590
Website: http://www.crf-usa.org
Facebook: @ConstitutionalRightsFoundation
Instagram and Twitter: @crfusa
The CRF seeks to instill in our nation's youth a deeper understanding of citizenship through values expressed in our Constitution and its Bill of Rights and to educate young people to become active and responsible participants in our society.

Electronic Frontier Foundation
815 Eddy Street
San Francisco, CA 94109
(415) 436-9333
Website: http://www.eff.org
Facebook: @eff
Twitter: @EFF
This nonprofit organization defends civil liberties in the digital world.

Foundation for Individual Rights in Education (FIRE)
510 Walnut Street, Suite 1250
Philadelphia, PA 19106
(215) 717-3473
Website: http://www.thefire.org
Facebook: @thefireorg
Twitter/YouTube: @TheFIREorg
FIRE's mission is to defend and sustain individual rights
    at America's colleges and universities. These rights
    include freedom of speech.

# FOR FURTHER READING

Abrams, Floyd. *The Soul of the First Amendment.* New Haven, CT: Yale University Press, 2017.

Ash, Timothy Garten. *Free Speech: Ten Principles for a Connected World.* New Haven, CT: Yale University Press, 2016.

Bradbury, Ray. *Fahrenheit 451* (Reissue edition). New York, NY: Simon & Schuster, 2014.

Cherminsky, Erwin, and Howard Gilman. *Free Speech on Campus.* New Haven, CT: Yale University Press, 2017.

Dudley, William. *Freedom of Speech.* Farmington Hills, MI: Greenhaven Press, 2005.

Green, Jonathon, and Nicholas Karolides. *Encyclopedia of Censorship.* New York, NY: Infobase, 2014.

Krull, Kathleen. *A Kids' Guide to America's Bill of Rights.* New York, NY: HarperCollins, 2015.

Mason, Jennifer. *Freedom of Speech.* New York, NY: Gareth Steven Publishing, 2017.

Safran, Verna. *Justin and the First Amendment.* Bloomington, IN: AuthorHouse, 2013.

Shipler, David. *Freedom of Speech: Mightier Than the Word.* New York, NY: Alfred A. Knopf, 2015.

ACLU. "Free Speech." Retrieved September 28, 2017. https://www.aclu.org/issues/free-speech.

Brown, Curt. "ACLU Wins Settlement for Sixth-Grader's Facebook Posting." *StarTribune*, March 25, 2014. http://www.startribune.com/minnewaska-student-wins-70k-from-school-over-facebook-post/252263751.

Comstock, Paul. "Eugene and the Fight for Free Speech." *California Literary Review*, June 26, 2008. http://calitreview.com/776/eugene-debs-and-the-fight-for-free-speech.

Constitutional Rights Foundation. "The Alien and Sedition Acts: Defining American Freedom." Retrieved September 28, 2017. http://www.crf-usa.org/bill-of-rights-in-action/bria-19-4-b-the-alien-and-sedition-acts-defining-american-freedom.html.

Epstein, Richard. "Do Armed Neo-Nazis Have First Amendment Rights to Protest?" *Newsweek*, August 29, 2017. http://www.newsweek.com/do-armed-neo-nazis-have-first-amendment-rights-protest-656443.

FindLaw. "Free Speech Lawsuits Involving Public Schools." Retrieved September 27, 2017. http://education.findlaw.com/student-rights/free-speech-lawsuits-involving-public-schools.html?version=2.

Goldberg, Eleanor. "Here Are 7 Petitions That Actually Moved the White House to Take Action." Huffington Post, February 25, 2014. https://www.huffingtonpost.com/2014/02/25/white-house-petitions-works_n_4848866.html.

Head, Thomas. "Freedom of Speech in the United States: A Short History." ThoughtCo, February 10, 2017. https://www.thoughtco.com/freedom-of-speech-in -united-states-721216.

Ito, Suzanne. "Protecting Outrageous, Offensive Speech." ACLU, October 6, 2010. https://www.aclu.org/blog /free-speech/protecting-outrageous-offensive-speech.

Klein, Christopher. "10 Literary Classics That Have Been Banned." History Channel, September 26, 2016. http:// www.history.com/news/history-lists/10-literary -classics-that-have-been-banned.

Knefel, John. "Grand Jury Rejects Indictment for Rap Lyrics." *Rolling Stone*, June 6, 2013. http://www .rollingstone.com/politics/news/grand-jury-rejects -indictment-of-teen-arrested-for-rap-lyrics-20130606.

Legal Information Institute. "Miller Vs. California." Retrieved September 28, 2017. https://www.law.cornell .edu/supremecourt/text/413/15.

Liptak, Adam. "Justices Rule for Protestors at Military Funerals." *New York Times*, March 2, 2011. http://www .nytimes.com/2011/03/03/us/03scotus.html.

Mason, Jennifer. *Freedom of Speech*. New York, NY: Gareth Stevens Publishing, 2017.

Pen America. "Defending Free Expression: A Toolkit for Writers and Readers." Retrieved September 28, 2017. https://pen.org/defending-free-expression-a-toolkit-for -writers-and-readers.

Rampell, Catherine. "A Chilling Study Shows How Hostile College Students Are Toward Free Speech." *Washington Post,* September 18, 2017. https://www .washingtonpost.com/opinions/a-chilling-study-shows

-how-hostile-college-students-are-toward-free
-speech/2017/09/18/cbb1a234-9ca8-11e7-9083
-fbfddf6804c2_story.html?utm_term=.31d31dbf063e.

Rechshaffen, Michael. "Comedians Ask 'Can We Take a Joke?' in a Documentary on Political Correctness." *LA Times*, July 28, 2016. http://www.latimes.com /entertainment/movies/la-et-mn-capsule-take-a-joke -review-20160725-snap-story.html.

Savage, David. "Supreme Court Rules the Slants May Trademark Their Name, Striking Down Law Banning Offensive Terms." *LA Times*, June 19, 2017. http:// www.latimes.com/politics/la-na-pol-court-slants -disparate-trademark-20170619-story.html.

Shipler, David. *Freedom of Speech: Mightier Than the Word.* New York, NY: Alfred A. Knopf, 2015.

Stuart, Reginald. "F.C.C. Acts to Restrict Indecent Pro-gramming." *New York Times*, April 17, 1987. www .nytimes.com/1987/04/17/arts/fcc-acts-to-restrict -indecent-programming.html.

United States Courts. "What Does Freedom of Speech Mean?" Retrieved September 28, 2017. http://www .uscourts.gov/about-federal-courts/educational -resources/about-educational-outreach/activity -resources/what-does.

Welch, Rodney. "Justice Alito Talks Free Speech, Invokes Dance-Rock at Dedication of USC Law School." *Free-Times*, September 15, 2017. https://www.free-times .com/news/local-and-state-news/justice-alito-talks -free-speech-invokes-dance-rock-at-dedication /article_17f40286-9a1a-11e7-849f-2f001928498b.html.

## A

Adams, John, 14, 15, 16, 18
*Adventures of Huckleberry Finn*, 34–35
Alien and Sedition Acts, 15–16, 18–19
Alien Registration Act, 19
Alito, Samuel, 8
American Civil Liberties Union (ACLU), 11, 24, 27, 28, 29, 30, 32, 40, 47, 51

## B

books, banning of, 33, 34–35
*Brandenburg v. Ohio*, 44–45

## C

Carlin, George, 9
*Chaplinsky v. State of New Hampshire*, 20
"clear and present danger," 11, 19, 30
comic books, banning of, 32, 35–37
Comics Code, 36
Comstock Act, 17

## D

D'Ambrosio, Cameron, 41–42

Debs, Eugene, 18, 19
draft cards, prohibition on burning, 12
dress codes, 26–28

## F

Federal Communications Commission, 20
"fighting words," 20
films, censorship of, 32, 37–38
First Amendment, 7, 9, 12, 14, 15, 17, 19, 20, 21, 23, 24, 31, 37, 40, 44, 48, 50, 53
flag, burning/desecration of, 12, 18, 44
Fortas, Abe, 24
Franklin, Benjamin, 9, 14
Fraser, Matthew, 24–25
Frederick, Joseph, 25–26

## H

Hamilton, Alexander, 14
Holmes, Oliver Wendell, 19

## J

Jefferson, Thomas, 14, 15, 16
Jehovah's Witnesses, 22
Johnson, Gregory Lee, 44

## ABOUT THE AUTHOR

Don Rauf is the author of multiple nonfiction books, including *Killer Lipstick and Other Spy Gadgets*, *American Inventions*, *The French and Indian War*, *The Rise and Fall of the Ottoman Empire*, *George Washington's Farewell Address*, *How George W. Bush Fought the Wars in Iraq and Afghanistan*, and *Historical Serial Killers*. He lives in Seattle with his wife, Monique, and son, Leo.

## PHOTO CREDITS

Cover Anadolu Agency/Getty Images; p. 5 Michael Zagaris /Getty Images; pp. 7, 14, 22, 32, 43 (background) KelseyJ /Shutterstock.com; p. 8 Anthony Pidgeon/Redferns/Getty Images; p. 10 Bloomberg/Getty Images; p. 12 The Sydney Morning Herald/Fairfax Media/Getty Images; p. 16 Everett - Art/Shutterstock .com; p. 17 Barcroft Media/Getty Images; p. 19 Apic/Retired /Hulton Archive/Getty Images; p. 23 Bettmann/Getty Images; p. 25 Bill Clark/CQ-Roll Call Group/Getty Images; pp. 27, 33 © AP Images; p. 29 Brendan O'Sullivan/Photolibrary/Getty Images; p. 35 Historical Picture Archive/Corbis Historical/Getty Images; p. 36 Thurston Hopkins/Hulton Archive/Getty Images; p. 38 Archive Photos/Getty Images; p. 41 Education Images /Universal Images Group/Getty Images; p. 43 Fred de Noyelle /Corbis Documentary/Getty Images; p. 46 Paul J. Richards/AFP /Getty Images; pp. 49, 51 NurPhoto/Getty Images.

Design: Michael Moy; Layout: Ellina Litmanovich; Editor: Amelie von Zumbusch; Photo Researcher: Karen Huang